G000167204

PARROTS
AND RELATED BIRDS

Rosemary Low

HAMLYN

Published 1986 by Hamlyn Publishing,
Bridge House, London Road, Twickenham, Middlesex

Copyright © Hamlyn Publishing 1986
a division of The Hamlyn Publishing Group Ltd

ISBN 0 600 30732 8
Printed in Italy

Some of the illustrations in this book are reproduced from other books
published by The Hamlyn Publishing Group Ltd

Contents

Introduction 4
Choosing and Buying 6
Species 13
Accommodation 17
Feeding 21
Handling 24
General Health 27
Breeding 31
Bibliography 31
Index 32

Introduction

Parrots and man have been linked together since ancient times. In the 5th century BC the Greek historian Ctesias accurately described a Plumhead Parrakeet – and this is probably the earliest surviving description of a parrot. In India, these birds were held sacred because of their ability to mimic human speech. The Romans prized them for the same reason and kept them in elaborate cages of silver, ivory and tortoiseshell, on occasion reputedly paying more for a talented 'talker' than for a slave.

Today parrots are still kept for their talking ability but are also appreciated for their intelligence and affectionate dispositions and for the beauty of their plumage. The parrots comprise one of the most colourful, varied and interesting avian families in existence.

Found throughout the tropics, the largest number of species occur in South America and in Australia. New Guinea, Indonesia and Asia are also richly endowed in parrots and there are a few species in Africa.

Many of the 300 species are bred in captivity or imported from the wild. The aim of this book is to describe some of those which make suitable pets and to offer advice on their care. If a wise choice is made a parrot becomes more than a pet; it can be a life-long companion of the most responsive and affectionate kind.

Grey Parrots are popular pets, particularly because they are unsurpassed mimics.

4

Choosing and Buying

Parrots make wonderful pets – but only in sympathetic and caring hands. It is also important that a suitable species is chosen. There are many species of parrots (this term covers all members of the parrot family – not only the short-tailed ones such as Amazons and the Grey Parrot) so it may be difficult for the first time buyer to choose wisely.

Where do you buy a parrot?
There are four possibilities: breeder, pet shop, importer and the private individual.

Breeders can be found by contacting the secretary of the local cage bird society (see page 30) or by reading advertisements in magazines such as *Cage and Aviary Birds* or *American Cage-Bird Magazine*. Pet shops are quickly located through the Yellow Pages – but not all sell parrots. Importers advertise in the various magazines but the birds they offer will be imported birds just out of quarantine. Only experienced parrot keepers should buy from this source. Local newspapers quite often carry advertisements in the classified 'Pets' column but beware of birds offered which have been bought as adults as they may prove impossible to tame.

Unless buying a tame adult bird which has already been kept as a pet, it is essential to purchase a young bird. With patience, most are readily tamed and some can be taught to mimic. This is impossible with adult birds which have not previously been kept as pets. Also, young birds settle down more quickly in a new home. Another factor to be considered is that the potential life span of members of the parrot family is much longer than most birds of comparable size. Amazons, Grey Parrots and cockatoos can live to 60 or 70 years and even smaller species like the Cockatiel often survive 20 years. As there is no way of ascertaining their age after they are about one year old, it is obviously wisest to buy one of known age. And this can usually only be a young bird.

How can you distinguish a young bird from an adult?

It is very important to find this out *before* setting out to buy a parrot. The number of people who have spent large sums on birds which they believe to be young but which are, in fact, adults is unfortunately high.

Characteristics of young birds differ according to the species. In some they are not easy for the beginner to discern; in others, such as the Grey Parrot, one of the most popular of all parrots, they are unmistakable. The iris of the young Grey's eye is dark, so that the eye looks black. In adult birds it is a clear pale yellow. An intermediate colour indicates that the bird is about ten months old and, in most cases, not too mature to tame.

In Amazon Parrots the eye colour changes at a much earlier age. By five or six months it may be nearly as bright as an adult. However, the plumage usually has a softer look, with more subtle colours.

In some birds, such as Cockatiels of the normal grey variety, there is a distinct immature plumage which is totally different to that of the adult male but resembles that of the adult female. The underside of the tail is barred with grey and yellow, whereas in adult males it is black. In young birds the tail is considerably shorter.

7

Orange-winged Amazon

Yellow-naped Amazon

In most species the distinction between adult and immature plumage is slight. However, any bird with a brilliantly coloured iris and horny and scaly feet is adult. Young birds have much smoother feet and in most species the iris is dark brown.

Blue-headed Pionus

Mealy Amazon

Wagler's Conure

9

How do you choose a bird?

The best choice is a young bird which is friendly and alert. If the bird is aviary-bred it should be in perfect plumage; if it is imported the plumage may be slightly imperfect as the result of travel and quarantine. Birds with missing tail and flight feathers should be avoided, especially cockatoos, as they may be suffering from an incurable feather disease. Beware of birds which are described as being 'in the moult'. In parrots the moult takes place over several weeks; it does not result in a bird being totally without feathers in any area of the body. Some imported parrots have their flight feathers cut. If this has been carried out properly most of the feathers will be replaced at the next moult when the parrot will then be able to fly. All that is involved is the cutting of some of the primary and perhaps some of the secondary wing feathers (flight feathers); if this is not carried out correctly, not only will the wing have a mutilated appearance but the unfortunate bird could be rendered permanently flightless.

When choosing a bird from a number which are in cages, stand back and study them. A bird under close scrutiny usually tightens up its feathers and appears temporarily alert because it has been disturbed. If it is unwell, it will, if observed from a distance, then assume a ruffled appearance, tuck its head into the feathers of its back and go to sleep. An adult which sleeps standing on two feet is normally unwell. Many young birds sleep in this way, however. It is important to observe the eye, which should be bright. A dull or sunken appearance is a sure indication of poor health. Check the eyes and nostrils for any sign of discharge – another sign of disease. Look at the feathers surrounding the vent. If these are stained or matted and the droppings are abnormal, the bird is probably sick.

Avoid birds which are excessively nervous. They will be more difficult to tame and may be adults. Also avoid birds which do not suit your circumstances – for example, if members of the family or very close neighbours do not tolerate loud noise, do not buy noisy birds like the Amazon Parrots.

Large birds

Many people yearn to have a big bird like a cockatoo or macaw for a household pet – yet few of these birds readily tolerate very close confinement. When they become sexually mature, at about four years old, their temperament may change for the worse. All parrots are extremely sociable and, unless they are so tame that they consider their closest human friend as their mate (which many do), they need to have the opportunity to breed. Many of those which are very tame are extremely demanding. If they do not have plenty of attention they scream incessantly. This often happens with cockatoos – the loud cries of the large species are almost impossible to tolerate indoors.

Another factor to be considered is that cockatoos and macaws have extremely powerful beaks and could wreck a room if left loose and unsupervised. Definitely not pets for the house-proud!

If you are offered a hand-reared bird, expect to pay more than for a parent-reared bird – and considerably more than for an imported bird. The fact that the bird is already tamed is reflected in the higher price. Hand-reared birds are irresistible; friendly and inquisitive they can be handled by anyone – initially. They may eventually show a preference for one member of the family.

Finally, ask exactly how your parrot has been fed and, if possible, take a sample of the food. Also note the position and type of food pots – some birds are reluctant to feed if the food receptacle differs from that which they are used to.

Noble Macaws, a species of dwarf macaw, make enchanting pets.

Species

Grey Parrots
Greys are the quietest of the large parrots. They have a pleasant range of whistling calls which, unlike Amazon Parrots, do not offend the ear. Greys are also unsurpassed mimics – they can mimic several members of the household with unerring accuracy. However, their one disadvantage is an unreliable temperament – few can be trusted not to bite when someone is obliging enough to scratch their head. Coloration: grey with a red tail. Length: 30 cm (12 in). From Africa.

Amazon Parrots
Several species of Amazon Parrots are suitable for pets. The Orange-winged, Blue-fronted and Yellow-fronted all have engaging personalities and many are excellent mimics. However, they are noisy birds that have regular periods of screaming, especially in the morning, which can be irritating and embarrassing.

Blue-fronted Amazon Coloration: mainly green but with red in wings and tail, a blue and yellow head and black beak. Length: 35.5–38 cm (14–15 in). From central South America.

Yellow-fronted Amazon Coloration: similar to Blue-fronted but with yellow on forehead and the beak horn coloured dark grey. Length: 33 cm (13 in). From Panama and northern South America.

Orange-winged Amazon Coloration: mainly green but with orange in wings and tail; head mauvish-blue and yellow; beak grey. Length: 30.5 cm (12 in). From northern and central South America.

Mealy Amazon Like many of the large parrots, the Mealy Amazon is best kept in pairs in an aviary. A wonderful mimic with a pleasing and gentle personality, it would make a perfect pet but for its size and extremely powerful voice which can carry half a mile. Coloration: mainly green with red in wings. Head colour variable (with yellow patch or a few red feathers) with greyish nape feathers margined in black. From northern South America.

Blue-headed Pionus These birds make delightful pets – they are very gentle and are quieter than the Amazons. Coloration: blue head and upper breast, usually with a few pink feathers on throat. Otherwise mainly green except for red under tail coverts and in tail. Black and pink beak. Length: 28 cm (11 in). From northern South America.

Macaws

Most macaws are not suitable for house pets because of their size – up to 0.9 m (3 ft); this includes the most well-known – the spectacular Scarlet and the Blue and Yellow Macaws. However, there are several species known as the dwarf macaws, such as the Noble Macaw, which do make enchanting pets.

Noble Macaw Coloration: mainly green, with bluish forehead, red and yellow underwings, a large area of bare white skin surrounding the eye and a black beak. Length: 30.5 cm (12 in), including long tail. From northern South America.

Conures
Members of this group (parrakeets from South and Central America) make noisy but engaging and intelligent pets if obtained young. One of the most attractive is the Wagler's Conure.

Wagler's or Red-fronted Conure Coloration: mainly green with red on forehead. Length: 35.5 cm (14 in), including long tail. From western South America.

Cockatoos
Like the macaws, cockatoos do not readily tolerate close confinement. Most of them are large and are not suitable for household pets. However, some of the smaller cockatoos are kept. They are friendly and tame, if bought young, but are not good at copying the human voice. They can also be very expensive.

Cockatiels
These delightful and affectionate birds make excellent pets. Kept in aviaries or cages, they are readily available in pet shops and from breeders. For more information see *Hamlyn Pet Guides Cockatiels* (in this series).

Senegal Parrot
One of the most popular parrots to come from Africa, some Senegals are very friendly, usually becoming quite attached to their owners. Although not particularly talkative, they may say some words or sentences. Can be kept in pairs as household pets. Coloration: mainly green, with grey head and orange underparts. Length: 23 cm (9 in). From central/western Africa.

Senegal Parrot

Blue-fronted Amazon

Accommodation

Cages When buying a parrot it is essential that they can be housed properly. Although most cages are expensive (large ones are very expensive) if looked after well they will last for years. It is therefore important that you should buy the largest cage you can afford from the outset. Alternatively, you can make your own.

Cages now being produced are much more attractive and hygienic than the traditional type of wire cage – which are square, difficult to clean properly and seldom large enough. An excellent design is one with a plastic base onto which the wire cage clips; it is therefore easy to clean. These cages are oblong, rather than square, thus giving the occupant more room. For example, a suitable cage for an Orange-winged Amazon should measure at least 61 × 38 × 61 cm (24 × 15 × 24 in). A cage of this size with a plastic base costs no more than a traditional type of cage measuring 46 × 46 × 61 cm (18 × 18 × 24 in). The type of cage to avoid are the tall, cylindrical ones.

Perches Commercially produced cages are equipped with perches which may be made of plastic or smooth wood. The plastic ones should be removed and the smooth wood perches supplemented by a branch cut from a tree. These are useful to nibble and gnaw on as well as providing exercise for the feet (if the thickness of the branch varies). Smooth perches can cause sores to develop on the underside of a parrot's feet.

Many deciduous trees, especially fruit trees, will provide suitable perching. Avoid branches from fir and laurel – elder is also unsuitable because the wood is too soft.

Food and water containers Those provided with cages are invariably too small and too few. Most cages have one of each. Three for food and one for water would be ideal, providing containers for large and small seed or nuts. The problem with buying additional pots which hook on to the cage wire is that most parrots delight in unhooking these and throwing the contents on the cage floor.

However, a recent development has been stainless steel coop cups which fit tightly into a wire hanger and can be hooked on the side of the cage. Larger than ordinary food containers, they are unbreakable and easy to clean – ideal for parrots. For the clever birds that can unhook them, a small padlock will prevent this.

Constructing a cage This is much easier than it might appear. Obtain two sheets of wire mesh (5 cm square or 7.5 × 2.5 cm) ready-cut – 61 cm (2 ft) square for top and bottom and four sheets measuring 61 × 91 cm (2 × 3 ft) for the sides. These can be welded together at a garage for a small cost. The whole should be very inexpensive and

A natural wood perch is preferable to smooth wood or plastic ones.

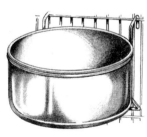

Above: a branch attached to a coffee table makes an attractive perch.
Left: stainless steel food/water container known as the coop cup.

will make a 61 × 61 × 91 cm (2 × 2 × 3 ft) cage, suitable for indoor use only. To house smaller birds than Amazon Parrots, please use 2.5 cm (1 in) square mesh. Cut out a 20 cm (10 in) square section for the door and secure with padlock – the larger parrots are adept at undoing doors. The cage can be placed on a block of wood, and newspaper put between it and the cage. Renewed daily, this is a quick and simple method of cleaning out. (Newspaper is also an ideal covering for the floor of an ordinary cage.)

Positioning the cage Give careful thought to the place where the cage is to be kept. It can be near a window, but not in front where draughts or sun could cause discomfort. Preferably, the bird should be in a corner at eye level, or higher, to give a feeling of security.

The most lived-in room in the house is the ideal location. If this is the kitchen, do not situate the cage near the cooker. Also bear in mind a vitally important fact: the fumes from a Teflon-coated pan which has been allowed to burn are lethal to birds.

New parrot owners often ask whether they should cover the cage at night. This is not necessary unless the occupant could be disturbed by lights from passing vehicles. Neither is it necessary to keep the central heating on for a parrot!

Cages with plastic bases are hygienic and easy to clean.

Feeding

Diet, exercise and fresh air are the most important factors in keeping your parrot healthy and, under normal circumstances, the most important of these is diet. An unbalanced diet, especially one deficient in vitamins, is one of the prime causes of ill health. The other is stress (see next chapter).

Unfortunately, parrots are categorized as seedeaters whereas, in fact, they are omnivorous, eating a wide variety of food items, especially fruits, vegetables and nuts.

Most parrots eat some seed and most of the large species are heavily dependent on sunflower. But seed should not form more than about 60 per cent of the diet of the larger parrots. In many of the smaller birds it forms a larger proportion – about 80 per cent. Seed is given mainly because it is convenient. If one of the larger parrots such as an Amazon or cockatoo ate no seed at all it would not matter provided that the diet consisted of healthy and nourishing items such as fruit, vegetables, breakfast cereal, wholemeal toast, cheese, egg-yolk, berries, such as those of elder and hawthorn, and rose hips.

All the parrots, excluding Cockatiels, normally kept as pets benefit from a diet that consists of 30 to 40 per cent fresh fruit and vegetables. Items offered can include apple, pear, grapes, orange, tangerine, banana and, for the smaller species, soaked sultanas. Many fruits in season can be offered; the favourites are usually cherries and pomegranates. Fruit should be cut into small pieces because many parrots are wasteful feeders; they take a bite and discard the rest. It should be offered in a separate container to the seed.

Suitable vegetables include carrot, cooked beetroot, celery, kale, cabbage, lettuce, peas (especially in the pod), green beans and sweet corn or corn on the cob.

Perhaps the biggest treat that can be offered to many birds is a branch of hawthorn berries. The hard kernel of the berry will be eaten (the soft outer part discarded) and the branch will be gnawed to shreds.

Also, cooked meat, fish and vegetables, eggs, cheese, toast, pasta, biscuits and fruit cake are all suitable and add variety to the diet. Avoid fatty foods, however.

Unlike many birds, members of the parrot family have well developed taste buds; this results in very definite likes and dislikes. They really enjoy their food. Variety is important not only to avoid monotony but because it reduces the likelihood of a deficiency of a vitamin or some other important component of the diet.

A bird which refuses all fruit and vegetable items is likely to suffer from a deficiency of one or more vitamins which predisposes it to diseases or problems such as eye disorders, paralysis of the feet and fungus infections. It is therefore advisable to offer one of the multi-vitamin preparations made specially for cage birds. This is not necessary for birds which eat items from the green-grocers.

For a single pet bird packeted parrot mixture can be used. When buying loose parrot mixture from a pet shop, make sure that it is fresh – if it is very dusty its nutritional value may be very low. Another source is buying from the large merchant by mail order, but do not buy more seed than will last for three months.

When giving sunflower seed to birds kept indoors soak the seed in water – it makes them cleaner and more palatable. If offered sprouted it is much more nutritious with a vitamin content many times higher than dry seed. It is ideal for those birds which refuse fruits and vegetables. When soaked seed is offered the container must be washed and emptied daily.

The larger parrots relish nuts – brazils, walnuts, hazelnuts, almonds, pine nuts and peanuts (beware, some carry harmful fungus). Peanuts are best bought from the pet shop or major supplier.

Also of interest are millet sprays, hemp, mung beans (soaked and allowed to germinate); smaller parrots, Cockatiels and conures can also be offered Budgerigar seed mixture (canary and millet) or white millet, canary seed, hemp and oats mixed.

Remember that your parrot enjoys a varied diet as much as you do – once you have introduced it to the items which are just a little more trouble to provide than seed!

Position food containers close to, but not directly below, the perch to help your parrot feed.

Handling

A common mistake is to try to handle an untamed parrot before it has settled down. This can set the taming process back many weeks. Some birds have a fear of hands and putting one's hand in the cage succeeds only in frightening them. In such cases they should be allowed to climb on top of the cage and will gain more confidence with each outing. Eventually, the day will usually come, even though it may take some months, when the parrot will go to the owner of its own accord. Remember then that the surest way to gain its affections is to gently scratch its head.

The most vital attributes for taming parrots are patience and sympathy. Without these, taming will be

Parrots can be handled only after their confidence has been gained.

impossible. Handling a parrot wearing a leather glove, as is sometimes recommended, is not the way to inspire confidence in a bird. Needless to say, rough movements and loud voices should never be used. Any form of cruelty can ruin a parrot's temperament and make it useless as a pet.

Many new owners make the mistake of trying to force their attentions on a parrot which is nervous initially. They do take some weeks or even months to settle down in a new home. The best form of communication is simply to sit by the cage and talk to the bird quietly as often as possible.

Teaching to talk If you want to teach your bird to talk, pick a simple phrase, such as 'come on', and repeat it as often as possible. Only one person, or people with similar

When first letting your parrot loose, let it come out on its own.

voices, should do this to start with and distracting sounds such as television or radio should not be competing with the parrot's attention. After it has mastered a few simple phrases it may learn phrases spoken by other members of the household or pick these up on its own. It may also mimic sounds heard frequently, such as a creaking door or a barking dog. It is advisable not to have the parrot in the same room as the telephone as some parrots can mimic its tone so faithfully that utter confusion results! On the subject of telephones, the most useful phrase that can be taught to any bird is its telephone number. Should it escape or be stolen this could be the means of its recovery.

Letting the bird out of the cage No parrot should be let out of its cage until a degree of rapport has been established between it and its owner. Unless so tame it can be easily picked up, it should have enough confidence to return to its cage on its own accord. Having to chase it destroys the relationship which is gradually being built up. If your parrot does get out of its cage and you have the type of cage with a removable base, unclip the base and place the cage over the parrot. If it gets out at night, simply note the bird's position, turn off the light and drop a folded towel over it. Hold it firmly because even small parrots can bite hard through a towel!

Before the parrot is let out, remember to remove or cover any hazards such as open-topped aquariums, pot plants which could be poisonous, dogs or cats which are jealous of the attention received by a pet parrot and, of course, open doors and windows. The tamest bird will take off if suddenly frightened. For this reason it should never be taken outdoors unless its wings are clipped.

General Health

Observation is an important part of looking after any bird. The owner should learn quite quickly how much food it normally eats in a day (food should always be in front of it – never rationed), the usual colour and consistency of its droppings and its sleeping habits. If a bird is unwell it will usually eat less (unless it has a problem connected with digestion of food), sleep more and its droppings may be an unusual colour or very watery. It will appear sleepy and listless. If you believe your bird to be ill, act quickly. The first step is to give it additional heat. Ordinary room temperature is inadequate for a sick bird. The most beneficial form of heat is the infra-red lamp produced for livestock. If one is not available, increase the temperature to about 29°C (85°F) and cover the cage with a towel. Consult a vet

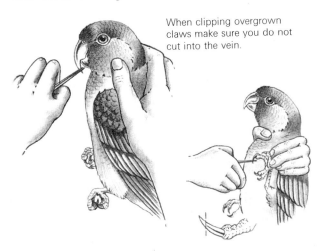

When clipping overgrown claws make sure you do not cut into the vein.

immediately, preferably one who is used to handling parrots. (Specialist vets are not easy to find.)

Many pet birds are lost because the owner fails to notice in time that the bird is unwell or to act quickly when this is realized. In many cases heat at the outset is all that is needed for recovery.

Most parrots are very healthy and remain so for years on end. Problems are most likely to occur with imported birds and during the few months following the quarantine period. Keeping your bird healthy and accident free is mainly a matter of common sense.

Stress Some species are more easily stressed than others – Greys and cockatoos more so than Amazon Parrots, for example. Stress in Grey Parrots can be caused by an action of such apparent insignificance that the owner is mystified as to what is wrong. Moving or changing the type of food container is an example, or moving the position of the cage. I have known a parrot to moult most of its flight feathers overnight as the result of being moved to another room – but normally stress does not manifest itself in such an obvious way. A bird that is stressed will be quieter than usual, lose its appetite and, most seriously, be much more susceptible to illness.

Depression Parrots can also suffer from depression, such as when separated from a much loved owner. They may even refuse to eat. Many family pets develop a preference for one person or for people of one sex – so if buying a bird which has already been part of a family, it is important to enquire whether it prefers men or women.

Aggressive behaviour Relationships between parrot and owner can become so strong that the owner takes the place of the bird's mate. The parrot may even feed and

An ordinary garden mist sprayer can be used to give your bird an enjoyable bath.

court its owner and behave very aggressively to anyone who approaches closely when it is perched on his or her hand or shoulder. Sometimes the aggression is so extreme that the parrot is no longer suitable as a pet. Often this happens when the bird reaches sexual maturity at three to five years old. The most satisfactory answer is to obtain a mate for it and give the pair the opportunity to breed. If this is impossible, consideration should be given to finding it a good home with a breeder.

Feather plucking A very common problem with parrots, especially African Greys, macaws and cockatoos is feather plucking. Again, this is usually the result of the bird being denied the opportunity to breed. If a mate can be provided before the habit becomes irreversible, there is every chance that the parrot will continue to lead a normal and happy life. If not it may remove its tail and flight feathers, be unable to fly and then become impossible to cure. Some Grey Parrots unfortunately denude themselves of every feather they can reach so that only the head is feathered. Every effort must be made to prevent this stage being reached.

Water One of the most important aspects of keeping your parrot in good plumage is access to water. Few will bathe in a cage, because the water container is not large enough. All birds kept indoors should therefore be sprayed at least twice a week (daily, if possible) with warm water. A plant mister is ideal for this purpose. Alternatively, you can even take your parrot in the shower! The gleaming plumage and the great enjoyment that water provides, will be ample recompense for the little time it takes.

Moult Parrots normally moult once a year, when all the feathers will be replaced, except possibly some of the flight feathers. If your parrot moults more often, the environment in which it is kept may be unsuitable in some way.

Remember that the amount of attention bestowed on your bird will be reflected in its health and happiness. It is entirely dependent on you. If you neglect it, its life will be one of misery. If you cherish it, it will become one of the family and its personality will blossom and develop.

You will be able to look after your parrot more efficiently if you meet other parrot keepers and/or read about other peoples' pets. Consider joining a local cage bird society or Parrot Society group (see local library), or joining the Parrot Society (19a De Parys Ave, Bedford) to receive the monthly magazine.

Breeding

Space does not permit covering the subject of breeding in this book. There are a number of good titles on the subject, ranging from those which cover all or many of the available species, to those which apply only to certain groups.

Bibliography

Hamlyn Pet Guides: Cockatiels by Dulcie Cooke (Hamlyn Publishing)
Keeping Parrots by Rosemary Low (Blandford Press)
Breeding Conures by Robbie Harris (TFH Publications)
Lovebirds, Their Care and Breeding by David Alderton (K & R Books)
The World of Macaws by Dieter Hoppe (TFH Publications)
Parrots, Their Care and Breeding by Rosemary Low (Blandford Press)
The World of Cockatoos by Karl Diefenbach (TFH Publications)
Lories and Lorikeets by Rosemary Low (Elek).

Index

Page numbers in *italic* refer to the illustrations

accommodation 17–20
Africa 4
African Grey Parrots 29–30
aggressive behaviour 28–9
Amazon Parrots 6, 7, 11, 13–14, 21, 28
American Caged Bird Magazine 6
Asia 4
Australia 4

Blue and Yellow Macaw 14
Blue-fronted Amazon 13, *16*
Blue-headed Pionus *9*, 14
breeders 6
breeding 29, 31
budgerigar seed mixture 23
buying 6–12

Cage and Aviary Birds 6
cage bird societies 30
cages 17, *20*
   cleaning out 19–20
   constructing 18–20
   positioning 20
choosing 6–12
claws, clipping *27*
cleaning out 19–20
Cockatiels 7, 15, 21, 23
Cockatoos 7, 10, 11, 15, 21, 28, 29
Conures 15, 23
Ctesias 4

depression 28
diet 21–3
dwarf macaws 14

eyes
   choosing birds 10
   disorders 22
   young birds 7, 8

feathers
   choosing birds 10, 11
   feather disease 10
   moulting 10, 28, 30
   plucking 29–30
   young birds 7–8
feeding 21–3
feet
   paralysis 22
   young birds 7
flight feathers 30
   cutting 10
food containers 12, 18, *19*, 23, 28
fruit 21–2
fungus infections 22

Grey Parrots *5*, 6, 7, 13, 28, 29–30

hand-reared birds 11–12
handling 24–5, *24*
health 27–30
heat treatment, sick birds 27–8

illness 27–30
imported birds 6, 28
India 4
Indonesia 4
infra-red lamps 27

letting parrots out 26
life expectancy 6–7

Macaws 11, *12*, 14, 29
Mealy Amazon *9*, 14
mimicry 25–6
moulting 10, 28, 30

New Guinea 4
Noble Macaw *12*, 14
nuts 23

Orange-winged Amazon *8*, 13, 17

paralysis of the feet 22
Parrakeets 4, 15
parrot mixture 22
Parrot Society 30
perches 17, *18*, *19*
pet shops 6
plumage *see* feathers
Plumhead Parrakeets 4

quarantine 28

Red-fronted Conure 15
Romans 4

Scarlet Macaw 14
seeds 21, 22–3
Senegal Parrots 15, *16*
sexual maturity 29
South America 4
species 13–15
spraying water *29*, 30
stress 21, 28
sunflower seeds 21, 23

tails, young birds 7
talking, teaching to 25–6
taming 24–5, *24*
telephones, imitating 26

vegetables 21–2
vets 27–8
vitamins 21, 22, 23

Wagler's Conure *9*, 15
water
   bathing 30
   spraying *29*, 30
water containers 18, *19*, 30

Yellow-fronted Amazon 13
Yellow-naped Amazon *8*
young birds 7–8